B

for your unmatched
beauty, curiosity, &
grind. your hustle will
never go unoticed, I
know you will manifest
all of your dreams.

WINNING YOUR RACE

Unconventional Truths from

a College Dropout

KHALIL SAADIQ

FOREWORD BY NATHANIEL SMITH

Thank you to the team at Niyah Press for their phenomenal editing services.

I would like to thank my family, the Society of Collegiate Black Men, and all members of the Omega Psi Phi Fraternity Incorporated for consistently molding and nurturing me from a child into a young man.

Thank you to Amarachi, Cam, Curry, Nate, Josh, Jerm, Jarvis, Korinn, and Jonathan for your unending patience, precious insight, and relentless accountability. None of this would be possible without you.

Thank you to the 5 Fatalities, for being my best friends and brothers despite seeing me at my worst. You all have pushed me to become my best.

This book is dedicated to all of us that have wanted to be **more** than what we already are.

ABOUT THE AUTHOR

-

Originally hailing from Birmingham, AL, Saadiq provides insight into his own life and endeavors, which took him from his hometown all the way to the United State's capital, while also allowing the reader to utilize his endeavors as a source of inspiration.

TABLE OF CONTENTS

FOREWORD

-

Nathaniel Smith, B.A. Public Relations,
School of Communications,Howard University

I met Khalil Saadiq in the fall of 2013, as new entrants of Howard University. From our introduction, I began to build an unspoken admiration and respect for Khalil that sometimes even approached envy.

Allow me to be completely clear with you; I do not have a jealous bone in my body. The thing is I had (and still have) never met a person with more conviction and self-determination, or a person who was able to elicit the absolute best out of every person that he encountered. Those were qualities that I had spent numerous years trying to find in myself, that he did with so much ease. Through our matriculation at Howard University, I watched as he captivated our peers while speaking at rallies and meetings, and how he could impact a person's entire being with one conversation.

After our initial introduction, we maintained brief contact for two years, both aware of the respect that we had for one another. I watched him closely, and was always blown away by the fact that Khalil never shied away from the trials and shortcomings of the University. Contrarily, he met them head on, as he does all of his obstacles. He did everything in his power to make it a better place not only for himself, but for all of his fellow students. I remember hearing a story where he personally went into a fellow student's room and fixed her window during the winter when her turmoil was overlooked by the staff. I couldn't help but think that his calling was higher than almost anyone I had ever met. In two short years, Khalil Saadiq became a memorable figure at one of the most prestigious universities in America, and had arguably one of the longest lasting impacts of any student in Howard University's 150-year history.

It is almost comical how the timing of people entering your life really has nothing to do with your own agenda. One day, Khalil confided in me how he would not be returning to school for the remainder of our Junior year. Oddly enough, this is when our relationship developed into one of the closest friendships that I have ever had. I was able to learn so much about myself, through learning about him. He made it obvious to me each and every day that he knew he had a higher purpose, and although we were both still finding ourselves, it became more and more clear that we would now be making this journey together, as brothers. He allowed me to understand his thought process in regards to the social and political climate at Howard, as well as the country itself.

I've never been more inspired to be my best self before meeting Khalil, and I'm thankful I was able to receive the gift. My self-confidence and belief increased with every conversation, for a number of reasons. One is because, even to this day he never allows me to be anything less than my best self. If I am not giving enough, he won't hesitate to say whatever is necessary to help me recenter and stay grounded. If I am doubting my ability or my vision, he makes it a point to remind me of my purpose and calling in this life, and for these things alone I am forever grateful. These usually take a person many long and difficult years to fully surface, and although we are both still learning and growing each day, the process becomes easier to embrace when you are constantly encouraged and expected to rise above it all.

Having confidence in yourself in knowing that your journey is your own is extremely important. I have witnessed first-hand how my best friend has been able to allow himself to make mistakes and be vulnerable, but also embrace overcoming his downfalls and finding the lessons in them that allowed him to become better from the trials. There's not many things that you can do to actually test the measure of a man, and you can usually only gauge him by how much he keeps his word. I would vouch for Khalil Saadiq's character one-thousand times over. Not claiming that he is perfect in any way, but I do not exaggerate in saying that he has been tested numerous times, and has always stayed true to himself and his principles.

We are all running our own race, but it is important to maintain faith through it all, and trust that your journey is your own and no one else's. *Winning Your Race* will equip you with the tools to uphold this mindset through every endeavor. Through the words enclosed in this book, we will all learn to have faith in ourselves, our own capabilities and perfect timing. In closing, I will offer you words from my best friend himself:

"Hope and pray is what most people do. Hope is like seeing the fire in front of you, praying for protection and then leaving it up to chance. It's inactive. Faith is sending up that same prayer, getting your mind right, and then taking a few steps back to give yourself a running start to jump over those flames."

HOW TO READ THIS BOOK

--

Do not read this book from cover to cover.
Please.
Don't.

Winning Your Race is not meant for anyone to read straight through. It is a series of chapters presenting scenarios that you're likely to encounter on your life's journey. Not all of them may apply to you (although I presume that most of the topics will).

Your decision to read this book is a testament to an important fact about you: You are serious about taking steps to successfully traverse the journey to becoming your best self. To help you benefit fully from the principles and practices presented in this book, I highly recommend that you consider adopting the following habits as you work through the process.

Of course, none of this is mandatory, but I strongly believe that these habits will help you optimize your experience as you apply what you read in this book:

- **Keep a journal.** In most articles describing the habits of successful people, you will find that they actively record their thoughts. I encourage *anyone* serious about their own personal growth to do the same. It will be immensely useful to record your thoughts so that you can accurately reflect, compare, and understand your feelings and perspectives at various times along your journey. A journal is also a prime place to record lists, goals, sporadic thoughts, ideas, and so much more. I recommend that you write in your journal at least once a week. At various points in the chapters that follow, you will be asked to write key pieces of information. Equip yourself with the right tools to make your objectives happen.

- **Adopt a policy of 100% honesty.** In this book, you will be asked a plethora of questions not only about yourself, but also about the people in your life and your past experiences. It is best if you make a silent pact with yourself to become brutally honest in your self-reflection. It is impossible to improve upon your current position if you do not accurately acknowledge what that position is.

- **Take your time.** Growth occurs exactly at the pace that it should. You may be in a place in your life where your circumstances require your full attention and then some. That is fine. The knowledge in this book isn't temporary. You must give yourself time to absorb the information, shift your perspective, and respond accordingly.

- **Judge yourself.** Your opinion of yourself is the only one that matters. Comparing your journey to that of others will only blur your perspective and discourage your progress. The *single most important* factor in your ability to gauge progress is your comparison to where you stood as a person the day before. If you can conquer yourself on a daily basis, your potential for growth is limitless.

- **Accept nothing at face value.** I heavily value the content in the chapters to follow. Nevertheless, I can only speak from my personal experience. Although I suggest methods that I strongly believe will work for you, you know yourself better than anyone and can judge for yourself whether these methods are best. Take nothing you read in this book (or anywhere else) as absolute until you have experienced the proof for yourself.

This book, like every other component of your journey, belongs to you. It has come into your life at a special time—the time you chose, in order to bring motivation, clarity, and guidance into your journey toward personal betterment. Take it exactly as you need it; there is no wrong or right way to progress so long as the steps you take are forward. I trust that you will find yourself challenged and encouraged by the things you find in the following pages.

INTRODUCTION: THE RACE

-

The journey that you are on in life is no simple one. You will face an infinite number of challenges and a surfeit of adversity. As you strive toward your life goals, you will realize a few crucial things about your journey. First, you don't have an eternity to achieve the things you want. You are only granted a set amount of time to live life, and you are racing against the clock to experience the most you can in your set amount of time. Second, this race is not a sprint. You won't excel in life by putting forth a high amount of effort for short periods of time. Your journey is nonstop; it is a marathon. Wise pacing is essential. Third, your only competition in this race is *you*. You can only justifiably compare yourself to your previous levels of performance. No one else, *not a single other person*, is running the same race as you. Comparing yourself to others is a waste of your efforts, and it doesn't give you an accurate idea of your own capabilities.

THE PATH YOU CHOOSE

You have options along your Race through life:

1. Path of least resistance. You can choose to travel the path of least resistance with little to no hardship. Your journey will not be eventful, it will not be challenging, and it will not be memorable. Along this path, you will find that your race requires little to no effort from you. However, you will not encounter anything scenic or worthwhile along the way. The entire journey will feel mediocre, at best.

2. The challenging path. This path will take you through life's mountainsides, treacherous gorges, barren deserts, and pleasant oases. You will face adversity of different types throughout the different phases of this race, but your sense of fulfillment and improvement will be second to none. This path, by its very nature, requires that you constantly strive to become the best version of yourself. If you are anything less than your best, this path will defeat you.

If, after reading the descriptions of these two paths, you decide that you would like to travel the path of least resistance, you can put this book down. You don't need to equip yourself with the knowledge presented here because you have no interest in becoming the best version of yourself.

On the other hand, if you read these descriptions and found yourself excited by the prospect of running life's race and pushing yourself to your maximum capabilities, then I greatly encourage you to read the remainder of this book. *Winning Your Race* tackles ideas of personal progression from a variety of perspectives, illuminating a surfeit of ideologies and tactics you can put into practice to continuously prevail in life's race.

The terrifyingly beautiful quality about life's race is its inevitable nature. Once you're in the race, you have to run until its conclusion. Since you find yourself on this journey, capitalize on the experience and reap all the benefits you can. The skills you can extract from this book will, once applied, render you a victor along every step of the race.

CHAPTER 1

DO IT
FOR YOU

I spent an exhaustingly long period of my life trying to fit in with others. I observed the people in my environment who were widely accepted and celebrated. I also could not help but see the vast differences in between myself and those social rock stars. This time in my life was full of mental, spiritual, and emotional fatigue. I was unhappy with my circumstances and unhappy with myself. I would go to extreme lengths to change things about myself—my wardrobe, my conversation, my haircut—to gain more acceptance from my peers. It never worked in my favor. In fact, it seemed to make things worse. I have never felt more isolated than when I was seeking the approval of others.

At a certain point, I realized that this had to change. I am not sure what pushed me to this particular realization. Maybe it was yet another romantic disappointment. It could have been a conflict between my siblings and me or an argument with a coworker. Regardless of the contributing reason, I suddenly found myself sitting in my parked car as I started home from work, realizing that I was not happy with the way a single component of my life was going. I had to make changes, drastic changes, as soon as possible.

I began to put myself first in all things. If I wanted to read for hours on a weekend instead of going out, I would do that. If I wanted to sit in the sauna at the gym for an excessively long period of time after a workout, I would do that. If I wanted to opt out of a conversation that I felt held no value for me, I would do just that. Most importantly: I never explained myself to anyone. I found that most people don't put themselves first, and so it is difficult to explain to them why I would want to do that, or that I was unhappy with things that seemed to be incredibly fulfilling for most people. Instead of burdening myself with attempting to break down the barriers of other people's misunderstanding, I would just leave that burden with them. It was a liberating process, cutting out all the things in my life that did not lend to my personal progression or satisfaction.

The *only* danger of relentlessly focusing on yourself and your own goals is that you run the risk of becoming overly indulgent, slothful, or unproductive altogether. I would always encourage you to live life while putting yourself first. However, there are some things you should keep in mind to avoid lapsing until a rut of self-destructive inactivity.

SELF-REFLECTION

"Examination of our past is never time-wasting. Reverberations from the past provide learning rubrics for living today."
−Kilroy J. Oldster, Author

Your romantic life is going well. Your new partner (well, your almost partner) is everything that your last one wasn't. And, more importantly, they are engaged with you. They seem to have an endless amount of appreciation for the things that you do and an unmatched depth that has you incredibly interested. Things are going phenomenally well.

And then it stops.

Your new partner (well, your almost partner) suddenly lapses into the same type of behavior that caused you to separate from your last partner. The situation is eerily similar, and you can't seem to figure out why you keep ending up with the same type of person that comes into your life. What's going on?

There are times when everything seems to be in order. The people in your life are proud of the work you've been doing. They acknowledge your efforts (which usually go unappreciated) and celebrate you for your accomplishments! Your social media accounts are teeming with interactions; your phone won't stop going off. The world is letting you know that you are doing well.

Once again, it stops.

The feeling of purpose dies down before you are able to create something new to gain the feeling back. It is not as if anything negative or detrimental happened; your momentum just seemed to fade away, and your sense of belonging went right with it. To make matters worse, you can't seem to come up with a way to get that feeling back.

What— is— going— on?

You have encountered some of the inevitable problems that arise when you feel as if you are lost in the world. Your internal compass is not working, and you cannot seem to form any solutions to solve the problems you face. Your self-reflection is lacking.

WHAT DOES SELF-REFLECTION REALLY MEAN?

Hundreds of commonly accepted philosophies are used to group people into different categories. Most of these philosophies are loosely based on Sigmund Freud's structural model of the psyche. Freud, an incredibly profound nineteenth century Austrian neurologist, categorized the "self" into principal parts. Freud's philosophy concerning the psyche of self is incredibly complex, but you don't have to understand it all to understand what it means to self-reflect. It is important to appreciate the foundational knowledge Freud offers, which says that you are a complex individual who possesses several components of your character that lead you to make decisions.

Therefore, if you don't take the time to actively look back on patterns of behavior and decisions in your life, you will find yourself in situations like the ones described above. Without proper insight, you may feel as if you are in the passenger seat of your own life and you do not control when you have high or low moments.

It takes time to effectively self-reflect. I encourage you to record your impressions in your journal; the insights you gain over time will be most helpful. Begin by asking yourself the following questions:

- When do I feel the happiest?
- When do I feel the most productive?

- What are my most fulfilling moments?
- What types of situations do I absolutely dread?
- What is currently my favorite place?

When you start your self-reflection process, focus on the *objective* components of yourself. Illuminate places where you were, times of day, and things you were doing that made you feel as if you were at your best. Once you have these objective things picked out, move on to a few more questions:

- What do my best moments say about me as a person?
- How are my best moments a reflection of my character?
- Are my best moments related just to me or to other people in my life?

These questions are much more difficult to answer, so it is important that you take your time. It is just as important that you don't receive any help from anyone in answering these questions. Developing a thorough, unbiased sense of self is a difficult and potentially daunting task, but it is *absolutely* necessary in order to reach a true sense of fulfillment and purpose in your daily life.

"Even if you think you're doing well and have it all figured out, there is a voice you will always inevitably hear at some point which nags at you and says, "but wait . . ." Don't ever dismiss it, listen to what it has to say. Life will never be close enough to perfect, and listening to that voice means stepping outside of yourself and considering your own wrongdoings and flaws."

–Ashly Lorenzana, Digital Content Creator

I'VE SELF-REFLECTED, NOW WHAT?

Once you have answered the self-reflection questions for yourself, you will have assembled a self-image, or an idea of yourself that is unique to you. This is where the real work begins.

You have to decide whether you like your self-image. If you do, then continue to practice active decision-making in order to re-create even better versions of those moments in which you felt your best. If you do not like your self-image, then it is time to start your journey toward your best self.

Identify the qualities in yourself that you do not like and identify the ones that you do like. Once you have done that, you can start to assemble a game plan to transform yourself from the person that you currently are into the person you would like to be.

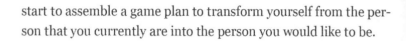

Successful relationships, successful careers, successful family lives, and success in general all share an underlying trait: they do not occur by accident. Only once you have an accurate self-image can you begin to understand what things work for you in life and what things do not. This practice will align you with your life's purpose and place you on your most important journey: the journey from the person you ARE to the person you would LIKE to become.

BEING CONSISTENT

"It's not what we do once in a while that shapes our lives. It's what we do consistently."
–Tony Robbins, Author

You set this incredible goal to get in shape. You wrote about it. You scheduled your gym visits. You grabbed an accountability partner. You told your closest friends. You are finally about to get in the best shape of your life and nothing is going to stop you this time. This time will be different.

Week One: You hit the gym hard. You're sore in all the right (and wrong) places, but you push through. You achieve all your gym goals for the week, and you get some incredible sleep to top it off. That weekend, you celebrate because you earned it.

*Week Two: Your soreness hasn't quite worn off the way you thought it would. By Wednesday, you are **exhausted**. You decide to take an un-scheduled day off, but still finish out the week. Your intensity is nothing like week one, but you feel good.*

Week Three: You go the gym about half as much as you did the first week. No matter which angle you stand at to flex your abs in the mirror, you aren't seeing progress. You just don't feel good about it anymore.

Week Four: Back to your life's routine before the gym ever came into the picture.

How many times have you done this? How many times are you going to do it before you realize that you have to make a change?

HOW DO YOU FIX IT?

Although you may never have had this exact scenario occur in your life, you almost certainly have set a goal and begun with great enthusiasm, only to have it fade away after a while. If so, you have problems with inconsistency.

Take a second to reflect on the various areas of your life where you can never seem to continuously produce the results that you would like. The gym, the workplace, the classroom, your relationships—all areas that will suffer greatly if you are not consistent. You seem to be trapped, living your life in between sporadic moments of high achievement that seem to be out of your control. If you find that you are inconsistent in certain areas, it is most likely because you lack discipline.

Popular culture has passively conditioned us to place value on natural talent over work ethic or dumb luck and incredible circumstances over hard work. For example, sportscasters frequently talk about Lebron James's incredible height and natural athleticism, but never his world-class training regimen or his intense willpower. This skewed focus gives us an inaccurate idea of what it takes to push ourselves in life. We shy away from things that do not come naturally, and we do not like to put a concentrated amount of work into accomplishing important tasks.

Developing your discipline is the key to being consistent and securing results in all aspects of your life.

"It's a marathon, not a sprint. Constant repetition is the path to progression."
—Nipsey Hussle, Hip-Hop Artist; Entrepreneur

Discipline is like a muscle. Without constant training, it will not work for you. Developing discipline is not as hard as you may think, but you have to start small. You would not run to the gym and try a brand-new workout with the heaviest weight possible; that would be dangerous and counterproductive. The same goes for discipline. Choose a small goal and a realistic time frame (it is generally suggested that it takes 21 days to develop a habit).

So, if your goal is to become more fit, then choose a task you can accomplish every day no matter what (e.g., *I will do 100 push-ups every night, no matter what. I will go for a walk every morning, no matter what*).

Attack this task without fail for your set time frame. No matter what circumstances present themselves, you *must* accomplish the task you selected. Do not make excuses. Set a relatively short time frame so that it is realistic that you can complete this task without fail. Once you have accomplished your goal, celebrate. Reward yourself with a gift or go on a mini-vacation. However you decide to do it, celebrate. This step is just as important as attacking your goal. If you do not reward *yourself* for your work, it will be difficult to motivate yourself when your situation becomes more adverse.

After this success? **Do more.** You have now seen what you are capable of accomplishing without fail. It is time to step it up. Now, instead of doing 100 push-ups a night, you do 100 push-ups and 100 sit-ups. Every—Single—Night. Set a new time frame. Accomplish your task. And reward yourself again once you have completed your new goal.

Just like adding more weight to an exercise you are used to in the gym, you will be able to accomplish more incredible tasks on a regular basis through your constantly growing discipline. Do not allow life's greater moments or the fulfillment of your purpose to escape you because you were not able to remain consistent on your journey. Whether you call it your grind, your hustle, or your daily routine, it does not matter. What does matter is that you are relentless in accomplishing the things that you resolve to do. Outwork yourself every day. Start small, and eventually you will see that even gargantuan tasks crumble beneath your unwavering discipline.

FEELING UNSATISFIED WITH YOUR LIFE

"People who are unable to motivate themselves must be content with mediocrity, no matter how impressive their other talents."
–Andrew Carnegie, Philanthropist

You wake up just moments before you have to start your day. You scramble to throw together an outfit that you're not excited to wear. You drink an energy drink that you know you shouldn't.

You leave the comfort of your home, which isn't as clean as you'd like, already anticipating the moment you'll get to come back.

You get back home and tidy up with the little energy you have left after your exhausting day. You stay up later than you should, distracted by social media or your "favorite" shows. Finally, you head to bed to get less sleep than you need for the next day.

You do this same thing every—single—day.

You work incredibly hard and never really see any results. You're caught in an endless cycle of mediocrity, boredom, and repetition. Your routine lacks fulfillment. And it's starting to eat away at you.

You can fondly recall a time when you were driven, excited, and passionate about the things you did every day! It was exhilarating. You were alive. But this isn't that.

HOW DO YOU FIX IT?

David Deida, author of quite a few remarkable books, has some powerful insight concerning the importance of finding your purpose:

Everything in your life, from your diet to your career, must be aligned with your purpose. If you know your purpose, your deepest desire, then the secret of success is to discipline your life so that you support your deepest purpose.

It seems unrealistic doesn't it? How is it possible that *everything* you do can relate to your life's purpose? How do you even discover your purpose?

Thankfully, your current situation is actually the first step in the process of becoming truly in tune with your purpose. The dissatisfaction you feel with your current circumstances is a sign that it is time to refocus on your purpose and move forward with your life.

It *is* okay to be dissatisfied with your current circumstances. It is *not* okay to allow your circumstances to remain this way! So, what steps should you take to get out of this rut and move forward?

1. Focus on things that make you feel productive: Whether it's cooking a meal or working out, completing tasks is essential for maintaining good energy. This positive energy will be essential in changing your situation around.

2. Identify the negative things in your situation: It is important to specifically identify the things that bother you about your day-to-day routine. It may help to write in your journal about the specific things you don't like. You can never fix anything if you don't know it's broken.

3. Develop an action plan: Each thing that makes you unhappy requires an achievable plan for fixing it. To fix your situation, it is important that you execute this part correctly. Results won't come overnight, but a better outlook and mind-set will.[1]

4. Set deadlines: Once you come up with plans to change some things around in your life, set deadlines, and post them in places where you'll see them every day. You might not always reach your deadlines, but seeing the dates is a great way to keep yourself on track.

5. Trust the process: Journaling is a recurring theme in self-improvement and tackling tough situations. Try to write down something you learn or something that made you happy every day while you are trying to change your circumstances. This practice will give you a powerfully positive perspective, an invaluable tool on your journey toward purpose-driven living.

Remember, it may not be easy to define what your life's purpose is. For some people, it is not as simple as playing basketball or writing songs. However, regardless of your passions, being the best version of yourself is ALWAYS a part of your purpose. Don't lose sight of being your best self, and never allow circumstances to define who you are!

Bad Plan: *I don't sleep well enough at night because my bed is uncomfortable. I can't afford a new bed, so I'll just deal with it.*

Good Plan: *I don't sleep well enough at night because my bed is uncomfortable. A new luxury mattress will cost me $2600. I can save $200 a week, plus any extra that I come up with, and I'll have a new mattress in 13 weeks!*

DEALING WITH FAILURE

"Failure should be our teacher, not our undertaker. Failure is delay, not defeat. It is a temporary detour, not a dead end. Failure is something we can avoid only by saying nothing, doing nothing, and being nothing."
–Denis Waitley, Author; Motivational Speaker

Failure typically is accompanied by some of the most hurtful emotions we ever experience. Disappointment, embarrassment, confusion, frustration, and outright anger, just to name a few. As we know, failure is an unavoidable part of anyone's journey to success.

So why are things this way? Why must we continue to deal with falling short of our goals? If failure is truly inevitable, why is it so painful?

The problem you have with failure isn't related to your ability, but your *perspective*. A simple shift in your mind-set can turn each of your failures into a victory.

HOW DO YOU FIX IT?

There is a **huge** problem with "failures" that many people never take the time to consider: you don't know what failure is. Initially, this may seem to be an ambiguous response to a specific issue. You're thinking, "Of course, I know what failure is. It's when I don't get what I want. It's when things don't go my way. It's when I work hard on something and can't produce the way I'd like to."

There is an abundance of reasons why you may put effort into something that doesn't yield the results you expected. However, there exists an even larger abundance of reasons why you still benefited immensely from the time and experience that went into the process you've deemed to be a failure.

The reason many people consider themselves or the things they do "failures" is because they lack context. Your life is a journey, and happiness is your destination. On your path, you will pass several landmarks and notable checkpoints, which you can deem as successes. However, this journey is not a straightforward trek from point A to point B, which would be simply unrealistic (and uneventful) to expect. Your goal is always to get from point A to point B, but your journey will undoubtedly be filled with all sorts of adversities, backtracking, detours, and dead ends. However, a traveler does not consider inconveniences along their journey to be failures. Instead, a traveler reflects on them fondly, often noting that "the journey is more rewarding than the destination." Life is the same way. The failures you encounter are minor inconveniences at most, only adding character, perspective, and insight to your journey toward becoming your best self.

"Success is stumbling from failure to failure with no loss of enthusiasm."
–Winston Churchill

Indeed, it is not easy to be accepting of certain failures while you are experiencing them. However, there are some simple steps you can take to keep things in perspective when you are faced with a tough failure:

1. **Focus on the lesson:** There is a lesson in every single failure. Even if, for example, you lose a race, you learn that to become the best, you must improve your training in order to run faster. With this newfound knowledge, you can adjust your regimen in order to reduce losses. Without this experience, you might never have learned this.

2. **Put it in perspective:** More often than not, we are only upset at failure because of our initial feelings of embarrassment or disappointment. However, a small dose of perspective can fix this. Ask yourself the following: Does this setback stop me from achieving my ultimate goal? Was working up to this point beneficial? Will I ever make the

mistakes I made here again? Typically, once you answer a few questions such as these, it becomes apparent that your "failure" wasn't such a negative experience after all.

3. **Keep moving forward:** It is easy to allow failures to slow us down, but once again, remember that you are on a journey to betterment and fulfillment. If you hit a dead end, you have to keep moving in another direction! You can take a break, but you must not stop moving forward. Stopping would give failure power over you and interrupt your journey. Do not allow yourself to dwell on failures and setbacks. Once you experience them, push yourself onward with renewed energy. You'll quickly see how your continuous progress produces results.

Failure is a natural and necessary part of success. Success without failure isn't commendable; it is luck. Embrace the hard times and adverse situations that your journey will bring you to; they only result in your improvement and a deepened appreciation of your eventual successes.

KEEPING THE MOTIVATION

"Never had to ask a lot 'cause I went and did it; If you lazy then I doubt that you would get it."
—LE$, Hip-Hop Artist

There are times when you find yourself in awkward phases of your life. You are proud of your past accomplishments, you are looking forward to achieving more in the future, but your "right now" just isn't so hot. You are not feeling that excitement, passion, or drive that usually propels you toward your goals. Your motivation is low, and you find yourself wanting to take a break from your routine.

These lulls in motivation can be incredibly dangerous for you when you're striving toward greater things. It is essential that you understand how to get past life's weary moments and continue to push yourself toward your ultimate purpose.

HOW DO YOU FIX IT?

The solution to low motivation lies first in facing the fact that your motivation is low and that you do not have time for this state of mind. So, let's get right on the ball with correcting this feeling:

1. **Take a small break:** At times, restoring your motivation is as simple as giving yourself time for rest and recovery. Athletes who work out heavily understand the importance of maintaining a sound diet and sleep schedule so their bodies can recover and deliver optimum performance for the next workout. Your need to recover your energy and motivation is no different. You must design a schedule that incorporates rest, relaxation, and recovery so that your energy and desire to work is replenished.

2. **Avoid Monotony:** It is difficult to strike a balance between establishing a routine by which you abide consistently and avoiding a lifestyle filled with bleak repetition. However, *difficult* is not the same as *impossible.* Consider the parallel example of an athlete heading to the gym after a hiatus. Assume that you have been tasked with performing 30 minutes of cardio each day. On one hand, you could go to the gym every day and use the treadmill for that allotted time. Would this accomplish your goal? Yes. Would it drive you crazy and drain you of your motivation? Hell, yes. However, if it kills your motivation, it is detrimental to the accomplishment of your goals. On the *other* hand, you could cycle one day, use the stairmaster another day, use the treadmill the next day, and then run outside on a different day. The variety in your productive activity will provide a huge aid in keeping monotony at bay, while allowing you to achieve your goal of 30 minutes of cardio each day.

Treat your personal goals the same way. Consistency is important, but variety may be equally important to keep your natural drive at its peak.

3. **Set the right pace:** When you're working hard, it is critical that you set up your planning so that you are able to work at your maximum capacity until your goal is accomplished. If you were at the gym, you would lift the heaviest weights first (after your warm-up, of course) while you had the most natural energy. You would save some of the more technique-based, lighter lifts for the end of your workout when your energy is depleted, but you are still capable of putting in work. You would take breaks between sets, but not breaks that are so long that you lost your will to work out in the first place! An effective workout is all about pacing. The effective accomplishment of your goals is the same way. If you have several tasks to accomplish in one day, try to punctuate the more tedious work with simple tasks that you can knock out quickly. Adding to your mental list of "Completed" tasks can provide a much-needed feeling of accomplishment that will motivate you to keep going throughout the day.

> **"Of course, motivation is not permanent. But then, neither is bathing; but it is something you should do on a regular basis."**
> —Zig Ziglar, Author

Another often overlooked component of motivation is positive self-affirmation. Positive self-affirmation is the **active** process of reminding yourself what you're capable of. Many people overlook the way they speak to themselves, if they speak to themselves at all. If you don't remind yourself that you're incredibly capable and that you deserve everything you working toward, then how can you expect anyone else to? It may feel silly at first, but once you start taking strides toward reminding yourself that you are on the right path toward greatness, even greater things will begin to manifest in your life.

Maintaining your motivation is a simple, easily forgotten task that will separate you from the masses. This practice will take your work ethic from "good" to "unbelievable" with the simple application of a few techniques. Imagine a vehicle that could fuel itself based on pure willpower. There are no boundaries to where it can travel. You are no different; be your own fuel.

SELF-DOUBT

"Believe in yourself, your abilities and your own potential. Never let self-doubt hold you captive. You are worthy of all that you dream of and hope for."
—Roy Bennett

> The feeling is all too familiar at this point. It strikes before you tackle any important task in your life: before you take a test, when you wonder if the new person you met is really into you, or after you submit an application for a new position. You begin to question yourself: "Why would they choose me? Did I really do enough to be here? Do I even really know what I am doing?"
>
> The list goes on, and no matter what you do, you can never truly silence the voice in your head that asks these nagging questions.

Self-Doubt can originate from anywhere, but it always seems to appear at moments when we need positive affirmation and encouragement the most. It is an ugly thing, one we can all do without. Self-doubt is the pest in the metaphorical orchard of your life, stealing away the fruits of your labor in the dark of night without your knowing.

To stop yourself from feeling inhibited at critical points along your journey, you have to set up your defense against self-doubt. Without a proper defense, doubt will steal your joy and your confidence.

HOW DO YOU FIX IT?

Self-doubt is most easily compared to the soreness that you feel after a strenuous workout. At times, it can be so severe that it discourages you from working out the next day. The intensity of the soreness, like self-doubt, can ruin your enthusiasm outright. However, there are other sides to this feeling. If you are able to overcome the soreness, you will find that your next work-out session is even more rewarding. In a strange way, you learn to embrace the soreness as a sort of testament to the effectiveness of your workout. Eventually, you reach a point where if you are not sore after a workout, you do not feel as if you have worked hard enough!

Your love for progress will allow you to change your perspective on work-out soreness and convey it in a new light. The same thing is possible with self-doubt. It is a natural occurrence, one that is near impossible to eliminate. But a shift in your perspective toward doubt can convey it in such a way that it becomes a positive tool for fueling your ambitions.

Once we accept our limits, we go beyond them.
–Albert Einstein

Picture yourself as a runner on life's marathon. Your path will change constantly and, at times, will be more adverse than others. Your self-doubts present themselves to you as hurdles along your journey, aiming to trip you up. However, once the doubts have manifested, you have no choice but to leap over them or allow them to impede your progress. We know what happens when you allow the doubts to impede your journey: you end up facing failure and disappointment. You will find your progress slowed to a crawl by hurdles manifested by your own self-doubt. There is no time for self-doubt along your journey.

Instead, compare this outcome to what happens when you leap over these hurdles of self-doubt and personal fears. The thrill of surpassing your own expectations is phenomenal fuel. Challenge yourself to confront your self-doubts with enthusiasm and determination and watch as they fall beneath you—no match for your sense of self and purpose.

Your journey is too important to allow roadblocks that you created to slow down your progress. Keep in mind that you will always be your first critic, and your most harsh. Remember that you are the only critic that you must prove wrong. Your self-doubts will always fall short of your consistent progression.

MAINTAINING A POSITIVE OUTLOOK

"Grow in happiness . . . and you'll glow in this peaceful way. Your friends will be very, very happy with you. Everyone will want to sit next to you. And people will give you money!"
–David Lynch, Filmmaker

"Is the glass half-empty or half-full?"

You've heard this question more times than you care to recall. Despite the time you've spent pondering this allegedly profound question about your perspective on life, you always conclude the same thing: you don't really care about this damned glass at all.

You do not see yourself as an optimist or a pessimist. You're a realist who takes things for exactly what they are. Or you don't honestly care enough to classify your worldview at all; you just want to make it from one day to the next.

*Of course, you're **supposed** to focus on the good things, count your blessings, and whatever else the self-proclaimed happiness-gurus recom-*

mend, but it's hard to see the point in this when the world is generally not a happy place. It's not particularly sad either, just annoying. It seems as if happiness is a by-product of luck, and most people just don't have a lot of that.

What if you were told that your happiness was your own personal responsibility? What if you could be as happy as you liked—all the time? What if your happiness was completely in your hands? Wouldn't you make sure your happiness stayed at great level?

You are the **only** factor responsible for your happiness.

MAKE YOUR LIFE A HAPPY ONE

People have quite a few common misconceptions about happiness, and thus, they go about maintaining their own happiness in all the wrong ways.

Here are just a few truths from Francois Lelord's *Hector and the Search for Happiness*:

- It is a mistake to think happiness is the goal.
- Making comparisons can ruin your happiness.
- Many people only see happiness in their future.
- Sometimes happiness is not knowing the whole story.

- Happiness is a certain way of seeing things.

Give yourself a moment to truly reflect on these truths concerning happiness. It is probably true that at many times in your life, you have made happiness a destination, thus removing it from your journey. You say to yourself: "Oh, when I'm promoted, I'll be happy." "Once I make it to Friday, everything will be fine." "I'll just lose some weight and things will be perfect!"

In these instances, you've deferred your own happiness, choosing to wait for an arbitrary point in time to claim your happiness instead of embracing it in the present moment. Practices such as these will always stop you from inviting positivity and healthy energy into your life.

It is important to realize that you have to undergo an active, intentional process to continuously manifest positivity in your life. Once you embark on this journey, it will bring happiness to your life in unforeseen amounts.

"Giving thanks, recognizing all the good in your life, is the gateway drug to a life most extraordinary. It's the superpower that moves you onto the frequency where beauty and joy and creativity happen."
—Pam Grout, author of *Thank and Grow Rich*

HOW CAN I START?

Remember, happiness and positivity are a process. Negative influences in life will always attempt to detract from your natural sense of satisfaction. To combat these negative influences, you must constantly remind yourself of the good things with which you are faced. Your journal is an excellent tool for helping you focus on the positives.

Every day, record at least one thing that made you happy in your journal. It can be as insignificant as getting off work early or as impactful as winning the lottery, but record something positive **every single day** (especially on your worst days). You will find that the *active* process of searching for positivity in your daily experiences is a tangible skill that can be honed just like playing an instrument. You will also find that, despite how it may seem, there is positivity in your life daily, and it cannot be avoided.

It is a hard truth to face for some—the truth that "all that positivity nonsense" isn't quite nonsense. It is also daunting to consider that you are solely responsible for your own happiness. Consider yourself during a time when you were happy and working; you were most likely alive with productive energy and fruitful passion. If you could have this level of enthusiasm all the time, your limits would fall away. The world belongs to those who love living in it.

CHAPTER 2

DO IT
FOR
THE LOVE

My introduction to heartbreak was laughably intense, given my young age. I absolutely adored a young woman who was also a classmate of mine. Over time, I discovered that the feelings were mutual, and the two of us became an item. During this time, all was well in my world. I spent entirely too much time texting, instant messaging, and talking on the phone with her. We exchanged thoughts, ideas, gifts, secrets, and all the other things people share when they are young and believe they are in love. However, there was a downfall to our otherwise magical relationship: she was hiding it from her parents. They were strongly religious and opposed to any kind of romantic involvement before marriage. This began to wear away at her conscience, eventually driving her to a breaking point. She felt as if she was forced to choose between religious salvation and her feelings for me. We decided that it would be better just to call off our "thing" and remain friends.

Despite my pride, I was distraught. My feelings were deeply involved, and to make matters much worse, we were about two weeks away from Valentine's Day. In my haste, I'd already purchased her gifts. Our school was having a Valentine's Day Dance, so I asked her if we could go to the dance as our last outing, despite having called it quits. She informed me that her parents forbade her from attending. I resigned my desires.

After much convincing from my friends, I decided to attend the dance and just enjoy a night out. At the time, it seemed like a much better alternative than sitting at home listening to Kanye's *808s & Heartbreak*. Upon arriving at the party, my friends greeted with me with matching grim expressions. They had no words, and I was taken aback by the lack of enthusiasm at my arrival. I soon discovered why they wore grim expressions: My ex was in the middle of the dance floor, enjoying an affectionate slow-dance with someone else!

Fortunately, I've long since recovered from this all-time romantic low. I believe that everyone has a story like this. For some reason or other, our romantic ventures seem to bear a great influence on our disposition at the time. People with successful romantic lives seem to be thriving and happy in general, and the opposite is just as true. Whether you're single, in a relationship, or not really looking for anything at all, there are a few crucial things you should keep in mind when navigating the emotionally intense landscapes of friendships, romance, and dating.

HIDDEN KEY TO RECEIVING AND GIVING YOUR BEST LOVE

"As I began to love myself I freed myself of anything that is no good for my health—food, people, things, situations, and everything that drew me down and away from myself. At first, I called this attitude a healthy egoism. Today I know it is 'LOVE OF ONESELF.'"
—Charlie Chaplin

The acts of giving and receiving love are colossal in nature. Although they are often described as coming "naturally" and "easy," these descriptions are incredibly misleading, as they do not take into consideration how heavily society influences our ability to love one another. To be able to give and accept healthy, wholesome love requires Olympic-level exercises in self-reflection, understanding, and patience. Giving and receiving love is not to be taken lightly.

On your journey to achieve an ideal love with your partner, you will face a multitude of hurdles. It is commendable that you would take the time to read more about the love you feel you already have or seek to obtain. So, take some time to congratulate yourself for that.

Perhaps, your constant desire to improve yourself and achieve more makes you feel as if, right now, you aren't good enough. You criticize yourself with incredible harshness (despite your successes and your amazing support group), and often don't feel as if you're doing as well as people think you are. You look at your progress and feel as if it isn't nearly enough.

Your ability to take pride in yourself and your journey is a direct reflection of your self-loving capabilities. If you cannot love yourself, how can you expect to love another?

You cannot. It is as simple as that.

SO ... HOW DO YOU FIX IT?

I encourage you to challenge yourself to reflect on your past relationships. Mostly terrible, right? You could easily list the flaws in your past partners and how bad their actions made you feel. Now, I challenge you even further: Shift the focus onto yourself.

For some reason, we are conditioned to spend our time and energy imagining, hoping, and dreaming about our ideal partner. Anyone we meet who comes close to the standards we've imagined, we immediately take on as our personal project. We task ourselves with taking a person, we mostly like, and trying to transform them into the person we could be with forever. This doesn't make sense.

This probably sounds idealistic or even naive. But it's time to stop focusing on the flaws in others and instead shine light on the person you are and, more importantly, the one you intend to become. It is difficult to have a conversation with yourself about self-love. Many people have never asked themselves key questions, such as these:

- Do I love myself?
- What do I love about myself?
- What *don't* I love about myself?
- Why?

If you've never asked yourself these questions, I encourage you to stop reading right now and do so. Write down your answers and give yourself some time to honestly reflect on your answers.

"Your task is not to seek for love, but merely to seek and find all the barriers within yourself that you have built against it."
–Jalaluddin Rumi, 13th Century Persian Poet & Philosopher

Once you ask yourself these questions, you'll quickly

realize how difficult it is to come up with answers that are satisfying. Why is that? Why is it hard to come up with things about yourself that you love? You spend more time with yourself than you do with anyone else; it only makes sense that you would love yourself deeply!

LOVING THE WRONG PARTS OF YOURSELF

We are constantly assaulted with influences that teach us to love certain things in people. Whether the focus is on a physical appearance, natural talent, class, status, it often falls on things that are out of our control. For example, an artist such as Alicia Keys is applauded for her talent but never for the humanitarian efforts that she leads in Africa. Or an athlete such as LeBron James is celebrated for his superhuman athleticism but never for his business smarts. People are often celebrated for things that they *cannot* control. If you allow these attributes to influence your perception of yourself, or of other people, then you can often draw conclusions about things that are misleading. When we think of ourselves, it is not with the same admiration that is given to celebrities or famous people we have grown to adore. *That's because we are only taught to admire external factors—factors that are often out of our control.*

Unfortunately, it is uncommon for people to celebrate attributes such as kindness, character, a giving spirit, work ethic, study habits, or any other factors that fall under a person's direct control. It is easy to forget about these characteristics—the ones that *really* matter.

Consider for a moment the reason that your mother loves you. It is not because you are tall or short, it is not because of your weight, it is not because of your money. It has never been about things such as those, and it never will be. She loves you because your mother, like everyone close to you, has had the opportunity to see you **as the person you really are**. Through your highest and lowest moments, the people close to you have been witnesses to your true character, and that has led them to love you. The people in your life, who have given you undying loyalty, endless sacrifice, and limitless patience love you because they've seen you at your most powerful as well as your most vulnerable. Through accurate self-reflection, you can achieve the same view of yourself.

LOVING OTHERS MORE THAN YOURSELF

Once you solidify this view of yourself, your new perspective will reveal where your energy should be going when it comes to romance. The reasons your past relationships have been unsatisfying are always founded in one truth: *You have been more loving to your partners than you have been to yourself.*

Shifting this approach will yield all the results you have been seeking in your love life. Consider how thoughtful, patient, forgiving, and attentive you have been with your romantic partners. If you were to take this same energy and focus it on your self-improvement, your opportunities would become endless. You will no longer seek things in others that you have not already provided for yourself. Once you immerse yourself in love for yourself, your ideal partner will present himself/herself seemingly out of nowhere.

It is nonsensical to expect others to know the way to love you when you do not know it yourself.

"how you love yourself is how you teach othersto love you"
−Rupi Kaur, Poet

Set aside time to spend with yourself. Meditate, be a little lazy, do ONLY the things that you like, shop, or listen to music. Discover yourself fully−better than anyone ever has before. Take whatever steps are necessary to achieve this. As you start to become more in tune with the person you are, you will begin to love yourself boundlessly. People who enter your life will have no choice but to reciprocate the love that you have for yourself, in full force.

"If you are waiting for anything in order to live and love without holding back, then you suffer. Every moment is the most important moment of your life."
–David Deida, Author

Think back to the days' when you've felt the best about yourself: Your outfit was perfect, your hair was immaculate, you ate your favorite meals, or accomplished challenging goals. When you felt as if you were at your best, you attracted the best. A little reflection on your personal experiences will prove this to be true time and time again.

I task you with giving *yourself* all the things that your past partners failed to give you. Immerse yourself into a world of self-care and self-improvement, and it will undoubtedly result in an abundance of self-love. Once you meet someone who treats you just as phenomenally as you treat yourself, you will know you have finally found a partner worth your time. Your flame is already lit, you just have to feed it.

As you run your race toward your goals and the best version of yourself, it is imperative that you grasp methods of giving and receiving love on your *own* terms. No one will ever be able to give you the kind of love you give yourself, and you will need that sort of love to conquer the adversity you will undoubtedly encounter along your race.

After you have accepted yourself, there is no end to what you can accomplish. By removing barriers between you and your truest self, you
eliminate the inhibitions that stop you from receiving the love from
others that you deserve.

EXPECTATION MANAGEMENT

"Expectations are dangerous when they are both too high and uninformed."
—Lionel Shriver, Author

Disappointment is one of the most universally dissatisfying emotions ever experienced. Whether you are disappointed in someone on something or someone is disappointed in you, the sensation is unpleasant and unfulfilling. Unlike sadness, grief, and even anger, which come in waves and lead to feelings of enlightenment or relief once they have passed, you are *never* glad that you were disappointed after the feeling has passed.

To avoid this annoying feeling, we must look to the root of it. Where does disappointment stem from? The answer is simple: expectations. Disappointment only occurs when expectations are not met. Expectations arrive from a plethora of places, but oftentimes, we are not aware of the root source of our disappointment. Many of our expectations are a tad unrealistic, maybe even nonsensical, when we take the time to give them more than superficial thought.

For example, when a man takes a woman out on a date and pays for dinner, he tends to think he is entitled to some form of physical intimacy afterward. Why? Similarly, women often do not expect men to match their level of emotional depth, and they tend to frown upon men who appear to be sensitive or in tune with their emotions. Why?

Many of our expectations, though commonly accepted, do not make much sense at all. Our rigid adherence to these expectations is what leads to nearly all our disappointments.

TAKE CONTROL OF YOUR EXPECTATIONS

Consider the example of two individuals standing side by side on a terribly rainy day. One is soaking wet—no umbrella, no coat, no form of protection from the rain. The other, in stark contrast, has rain boots, a poncho, and an umbrella, staying as dry as possible. The first individual (the one who is drenched) is disappointed. That person obviously did not expect to be faced with a torrential downpour. The **reason** they did not expect this downpour is because they did not put in the effort to *manage their expectations.* If they had taken the time to check the forecast (like the prepared, dry individual in the scenario) or even to glance at the sky before heading out for the day, they would have seen factors leading them to expect rain. Instead, they neglected to take control of their expectations and faced severe disappointment as a result.

Taking control of your expectations is nearly always as straightforward as checking the forecast or glancing at the sky, but there are some key things to remember about the process.

1. **Question the source of your expectations.** Taking control of your expectations starts with questioning why you form them in the first place. Initially, this will be harder than it sounds. Many of our expectations come to us almost instinctively, the result of years of conditioning that we have never challenged. The next time that you are disappointed with someone's actions, question your own expectations before you project disdain at the offending person.

   Hypothetically speaking, you may be disappointed that your friend did not call you on your birthday. However, upon your reflection, you remember that this friend has *never* called except to gossip, invite you out, or ask you for something. So, it does not really make sense that you expected to receive a birthday phone call. It makes way more sense that you would start looking for new friends! Questioning the source of your expectations will lead you to numerous conclusions such as this and provide you with a new level of clarity that will benefit your life.

"Expectations are like fine pottery. The harder you hold them, the more likely they are to crack."
–Brandon Sanderson, Author

2. **Do not confuse expecting with condoning.** This concept can be a bit confusing, so let's use an example to provide clarity. Consider that you have met a new person that you are interested in, and upon asking your friends about this person of interest, you are informed that the person has a track record of infidelity in their relationships. (This is the *precise* moment where most people fail to manage their expectations and proceed accordingly; so pay close attention.) In this instance, if you were to date the person, that is perfectly acceptable, so long as you adequately prepare yourself for what may happen if they exhibit the infidelity as you have been forewarned. Consider the previous example of venturing out into the storm: your "forecast" is your friends' warning that this person has a history of infidelity, and your coat, boots, and umbrella are the appropriate levels of caution and wariness that you display based on your forecast.

   What is important here is to understand a critical factor: *Just because you proceeded into the storm well-prepared does not mean that you asked for the rain.* Many people spend their energy aggressively hoping for certain outcomes. They do not take the time to prepare for alternative situations because they have so hoped for a certain one to unfold. Just because you have accepted that a negative outcome is likely does not mean that you condone it. Take the time to consider the reality of *every* situation that you are entering, so that you can handle whatever circumstance it may present you.

Once you get into the habit of examining and managing your expectations, you will begin to take control of your life in a way that your peers may think is abnormal, even mystical. As you tackle your journey toward the fulfillment of your goals, you will be faced with incredible adversity. You have no control over this, but you *do* have control over the amount of preparation you take before encountering any hardship. Effective expectation management will allow you to avoid the disappointment of unforeseen, undesirable circumstances.

The time you take to manage your expectations will only create more time for you to work toward more desirable outcomes. There are two generally accepted solutions to creating more happiness: lowering your expectations or improving your reality. Expectation management will help you achieve the latter.

BEING VULNERABLE

"To share your weakness is to make yourself vulnerable; to make yourself vulnerable is to show your strength."
—Criss Jami, Poet

Take a few minutes to recall your most embarrassing moment. Whether it was professing your love for someone who did not return those feelings for you or working incredibly hard on something only to have it fail miserably in front of people. These situations share a common factor: In that moment, you were completely vulnerable. At times such as these, we have no barrier between our true selves and the rest of the world. Because of that, our feelings become heightened, and all our emotions our amplified.

When we reflect on the times when we exposed ourselves to the world, it can cause us to grimace. The mere thought of being sincere with strangers is terrifying and does not evoke any positive emotions. Upon your initial reflection, it may not seem like any good came from your vulnerability, especially when "strong people" are usually described as lacking any vulnerabilities or weaknesses. What good do you *really* have to gain from being vulnerable?

Contrary to popular opinion, some of your most incredible experiences stem from moments of pure, honest vulnerability. Take a moment to think back on your childhood when you were able to immerse yourself in uninterrupted joy, with no fear of judgement. You experienced the most incredible feelings of satisfaction, as there were *no barriers between you and the world.* Think again to those times when you emerged as the victor in a fierce competition, finally earning the reward you worked so hard for. That moment of success was a moment of vulnerability, where nothing stood between the world and your desire to emerge as a victor.

Although it is difficult to imagine, vulnerability, a quality we fight so hard to contain and hide, can be a source of profound strength.

THE POWER IN BEING EXPOSED

Your decision to remain proud and true to yourself, despite being vulnerable, removes the power that negative influences have over you. It returns control of your circumstances to you where it belongs.

For most of your life, you have most likely been conditioned to put up a barrier between the world and your true self because you would like to make the right impression. For example, we do not reveal how we truly feel when we are at job interviews or on first dates or in large social settings. Why? We are paralyzed by the thought that we may reveal a portion of ourselves to the world and that the world will not approve of us.

Now, reflect with clarity on moments when you have chosen to neglect this conditioning. Instead of hiding your true self, you chose to hold nothing back. This may have come during a performance, a competition, or a confession of your love to a romantic partner. These moments usually stem from high-pressure situations in which your instincts took over and you decided to do the unthinkable: Be yourself.

In some of these instances, we do not get the results that we want. In others, things go miraculously well, better than we ever could have expected. In both instances, however, we are not left with feelings of regret once the situation concludes. We do not look back on these moments and think of all the things we *could, should,* or *would* have said or done because we did them all! You can finally take comfort in your actions and embrace life's outcomes because you know that you remained true to yourself and earned whatever results you received.

"Vulnerability is the birthplace of love, belonging, joy, courage, empathy, and creativity. It is the source of hope, empathy, accountability, and authenticity. If we want greater clarity in our purpose and more meaningful, spiritual lives, vulnerability is the path."
—Brene Brown, Author

WHEN KEEPING IT REAL GOES WRONG

It is important to embrace your own vulnerabilities and share them with the people closest to you; however, it is just as important to utilize your discretion in deciding who to share these portions of yourself with and when you share them.

- **Timing.** In some instances, the timing in which you decide to share a vulnerability can make a profound difference in its impact. Say you are at work and your boss assigns you a daunting project. You know that this project may require things that are outside of your skill set, and you are concerned about your ability to complete the project alone. You can take either of two courses of action. On one hand, as soon as you are assigned the project, you could express your concerns to your boss. She will likely decide to give the project to someone else, and you will have missed an opportunity to better yourself and perform exceptional work. On the other hand, you could wait until *after* you have completed the project to a satisfactory level before sharing your concern with your boss. Upon hearing that you felt underprepared for this project, your boss will likely be immensely impressed with your decision to tackle it anyway. In this case, your boss commends you and agrees to give you more responsibility in the future in order to expand your skill set, which is obviously being underutilized!

- **Overdoing It.** Understand this: Embracing your own vulnerability does not mean that you volunteer exactly how you feel about a given situation simply because it presents itself. Vulnerability does not always equate to an outpouring of emotions; it is much simpler than that. Vulnerability is admitting that you have never heard of something when someone assumes that you have. Vulnerability is asking the question even though some would call it a "stupid question." Vulnerability is admitting when you are wrong. Vulnerability is accepting things about yourself and having no fear in revealing those things to others. There are times when we do not want to do certain things for fear of how they will make us look. We need to outgrow this fear and embrace whatever comes as a result of doing the things we want to do.

Vulnerability is no simple thing to demand of yourself. It takes an incredible amount of self-trust and self-acceptance to be comfortable revealing things others would consider shortcomings. However, once you make a habit of doing so, you will find yourself with a level of empowerment unmatched by anything you have felt before. Once you have chosen to share your true self with the world, nothing is off limits to you.

GETTING TO KNOW ONE ANOTHER

"Build a bond first, don't force anything. A person's actions will tell you everything you need to know."
—40oz Van, Digital Content Creator, Social Influencer

> You've met this person and, from the outside looking in, they seem to meet **all** your requirements. They are attractive, they make great conversation and, most importantly, they seem to be just as interested in you as you are in them. But, you are unsure of what to do next. You think you have a real chance at something special with this person. No matter what, you do not want this time to go like the last time you invested energy in a person.

Plenty of times, we find ourselves caught in the incredibly awkward phase between becoming interested in a person and establishing an actual foundation. It is a tricky space to navigate, and it can last for weeks, months, or even years. Whether you call it "talking," "courting," "dating," or any other variation of the term, the only goal of this phase is to determine whether your *interest* and *attraction* to a person is enough to warrant anything substantial or long-term.

But what do you fill this space with? How do you find ways to interact with a person without ruining the mutual interest that you have? How do you progress from being two individuals into a duo that is "official" and can withstand difficult circumstances?

How do you ensure that you will not waste time with this person like you did the last time you met someone who seemed "right"?

SPENDING THE RIGHT KIND OF TIME TOGETHER

The most important component of getting to know a person is establishing comfort. If you cannot create a level of comfort with your potential partner, then the relationship most likely will not work. You have to spend the right kind of time with a person in order to accomplish this. There are a couple of scenarios that work well universally to build bonds. These are just a few of several great ways to get to know a potential partner:

- **The Lunch Date:** This is undoubtedly one of the most useful ways to have profound dialogue with a person. Dinner dates are accompanied by a plethora of unspoken expectations. They occur in the evening, which often strongly implies that some form of intimacy is expected. This can be uncomfortable for both parties. Dinner also tends to be more expensive than any other meal of the day. Even if your dinner results in amazing conversation, if it occurs late at night, it will have to be cut short because the two of you may not be comfortable enough with one another to spend late evenings together.

The lunch date, on the other hand, solves all these problems. First off, it is less expensive than dinner, so if you are planning to pay for two people to eat, then you can usually save money. Second, the time of day allows both parties to relax easily. When you can spend time with another person, free of expectations, it promotes a more relaxed atmosphere. You can converse without fear of being judged and without regrets because ultimately, lunch is harmless, right? If lunch goes well, it is simple enough to spend even more time together right after lunch, or even later that evening. Whatever the outcome, lunch dates provide an ideal opportunity to build comfort with another person in a casual environment.

- **The Shared Activity:** For some reason, when getting to know a person, we often want to do something with them that we would never normally do. We think it is a good idea to go bowling, see a movie, visit a museum, or any other cliché activity that budding couples partake in. *This does not make sense.* Why would you choose an activity that you typically have no interest in doing and expect to have a good time with a person you are not entirely familiar with yet? Instead, invite them to do something you do anyway! If you take a yoga class that you enjoy once a week, invite your potential partner there. If you visit your local library often, invite your potential partner there with you. If you and your potential partner are able to share the positive energy and joy that you get from your passions, it is a great sign that you two will work well together.

The **bottom line** to draw from these scenarios is that it is in poor taste to step too far outside of yourself when getting to know a person. Instead, seek to learn how well that person fits into your current lifestyle (especially when you are fond of it). If you find yourself doing things that do not come naturally to you in order to date a person, then you will soon find yourself in a relationship that feels *just* as unnatural. None of this will benefit you.

"Authenticity is a collection of choices that we have to make every day. The choice to let our true selves be seen."
−Brene Brown, Author

For some reason, when seeking to get to know a person, we have a terrible habit of sending our "authorized representative" to impress them. You polish yourself to an abnormal level, try to go somewhere you do not normally go, and even eat foods you would not normally eat to impress this new person who has gained your attention. There is no sense of authenticity or truth in this method. It will fail, not only because you are not being true to yourself, but also because you will inevitably grow exhausted of maintaining the facade. This is not fair to your potential partner, who will wonder why you seem different after a few weeks or months, nor is it fair to you to ever feel as if you have to suppress your true self in order to build a bond with anyone. Take the time to introduce your potential partner to your world, one step at a time. If the bond you two establish is authentic, it will develop easily and without mixed emotion. I would encourage you to abandon all the generalizations and preconceived ideas you have about dating and instead look at dating as an extended compatibility test that **does not** interrupt your regularly scheduled, productive routine.

When your lifestyle is focused on your personal development and betterment, it does not make sense to interrupt that for a person who shows strong potential. Anyone or anything can show strong potential if your imagination is active enough. I encourage you to take a more realistic, casual approach to getting to know your potential partners so that you can reap the benefits of authentic romantic bonds.

THE FEELING OF SETTLING

"There is no more miserable human being than one in whom nothing is habitual but indecision."
–William James, Philosopher

You've found yourself in great situation with your romantic partner. Things are going as well as you could have imagined. The dates are fun, the intimacy is there, you get along with one another's families; you have no complaints!

However, . . . You can't shake this feeling of uneasiness. You're not sure what it stems from.

Is there something missing? Could the person be doing more? Is there a better person for you?

This is not the first time you've battled with this underlying anxiety in a situation like this—a situation where nothing seems to be going wrong, but you're still not sure if everything is right.

You wonder if you're settling in your romantic life.

THE SETTLING ANXIETY

It is difficult to vanquish the constant anxiety that tends to nag at you once you enter romantic situations. We'll call this sensation "the Settling Anxiety." It's a voice that says to you, *"This is nice, but it could be better, right? Don't you think there's better for you? Maybe being single was more fun."* The Settling Anxiety leaks into previously satisfying situations and ruins your sense of contentment. If this is not handled correctly, it can have disastrous implications for you and your partner.

WHAT NOT TO DO:

1. **Ignore it:** Unfortunately, the Settling Anxiety is not something you can just overlook and hope that it passes. It is infectious and persistent. Once it seeps in, it begins to stain your perception of your entire relationship. To get past Settling Anxiety, your feelings must be addressed.

2. **Look for external solutions:** It is a natural urge to look for solutions from outside sources to resolve problems occurring within your relationship. Although this may initially seem sensible, it only results in disaster when dealing with the Settling Anxiety. In most cases, if you communicate to an external observer that you feel as if you're settling in your relationship, they will most likely agree because they want what is best for you. Any advice you seek about your

relationship from an outside source is likely to be biased in your favor, and that does not mix well with the Settling Anxiety because it removes the responsibility from you entirely.

3. **Blame your partner:** This option is guaranteed to ruin any great relationship, and it is a terrible habit for a person to adopt in general when it comes to maintaining a successful romantic life. Understand this about the Settling Anxiety: If you were once content with a person and then over time you find yourself wanting more, then YOU are the reason for this feeling, not your partner. Self-reflection and open communication will be the keys to solving this problem, not the blame game.

"Allow people to know your wants, needs and desires in their most natural form."
–Diamond Dorris, Digital Content Producer

Fortunately, there are steps you can take to shake off the Settling Anxiety. For any of these steps to work, you must fully accept responsibility. Once you accept that it is your job to eliminate the feeling, you will find it easier to reach a solution.

• **Identify what you are missing:** Often, simply taking the time to reflect and identify specific things that your relationship lacks will guide you toward the solution. A transparent, straightforward conversation with your significant other can yield profound results for a situation such as this and put the two of you on the path to ridding you of the Settling Anxiety. If identifying the solution proves difficult, remember to look inward. You may be missing something in your life that you are projecting onto your partner unknowingly.

- **Involve your partner:** There are some issues that you may not want to share with your partner once you discover them. Maybe you still want to enjoy nightlife or maybe you don't find yourself as physically attracted to your partner as you once were, and your love life lacks that certain "spark." In both cases, it may be uncomfortable to express these things to your partner directly. However, taking the opposite course can yield outstanding results. For example, invite your partner to enjoy your favorite bar or club with you, so that the two of you can share the experience you find yourself missing. Challenge your partner to get a gym membership with you, so that you both may work on improving your physiques. The possibilities are endless, and better results will produce themselves when you include your partner in the process.

You may encounter that rare case in which, despite your best efforts, you are not able to identify reason for your Settling Anxiety. In this case, the only advisable course of action is to have a direct conversation with your partner. The conversation won't be easy, but it will lead you to a better course of action. Throughout these moments of challenging dialogue, keep two key things in mind: (1) your partner wants what's best for you, and (2) everything was fine until *you* developed these feelings. The latter portion of this sentence is not meant to place blame, but instead to encourage you to proceed with every intention of eliminating the Settling Anxiety because since it came from you, it will have to be solved by you.

Unfortunately, when it comes to unique feelings such as the Settling Anxiety, there is no one-size-fits-all solution. At times, many things won't seem to work. However, once you are fully in tune with yourself, you will always be able to identify why you feel certain things. Self-reflection is always a great first step. The adversity that you and your partner face and conquer will certainly strengthen your bond.

BREAKING UP

"The truth will set you free, but first it'll piss you off."
−Pharrell, Recording Artist

Everything was going great just three months ago. You met this amazing person who you spent hours talking with every day.

You two went on amazing dates, loved the same movies, were annoyed by the same things, shared secrets, and had amazing physical chemistry to top it all off.

You went completely against the grain and rushed right into a full-blown relationship with this seemingly wonderful person! And now?

Things are terrible for you. Nothing is going how you expected it to. Your shared interests and the mutual feelings you had are no longer enough for you to overlook this person's problematic ways.

You know you must make a change, and soon

(your sanity is on the line.) But, even though they aren't making you happy anymore, you don't want to hurt your partner.

HOW DO YOU FIX IT?

It is key to remember one rule when navigating through romantic situations: put yourself first. To most, that may seem counterintuitive to the goal of the relationship. However, that misconception stems from a misunderstanding of what it takes to truly be successful in any relationship; that is, you must be the best possible version of yourself in order to give and receive love from another. A partner who does not allow you to become your best self will **never** work out in the long term, despite having strong feelings for you.

Consider for a moment that becoming your best self is like assembling a puzzle. You and your partner are like two puzzle pieces that appear to fit together. When you two unite, everything seems to work perfectly. However, as more of the puzzle pieces come together around you, it starts to become clear that the two of you only *appear* to fit together, but you don't belong near one another at all! The enthusiasm that you felt because of the initial chemistry caused you to overlook the big picture, the end goal, the *whole point*. It is **never** worth sacrificing the integrity of the big picture for two small pieces that don't belong together.

> *"Care about what other people think and you will always be their prisoner."*
>
> —Lao Tzu, Philosopher

When you step back and focus on the big picture, it's easy to see how important it is to cut off this toxic relationship you're in, despite the possibility of hurting your partner. These approaches can make the process easier:

- **Honest Conversation:** This may be the most effective, albeit the most difficult, method for ending the relationship. Simply tell your partner that you feel spending time with them is stopping your growth as a person. Encourage a friendship afterwards, and even suggest the possibility of a relationship in the future. Regardless whether that *could* happen, it's apparent that what is happening *now* isn't working, and you both need to take steps back from it.

- **The Letter:** It is difficult to tell someone that they aren't meeting your needs face-to-face. But it is important, for their growth and your peace of mind, that you communicate these things in some way. It may help to write a letter detailing the decision that you've made and why, give them some time, and then have a conversation about the situation when feelings are less raw and emotions aren't as high.

Whatever plan of action you take, remember that clear and effective communication is not only recommended, but it is required for a decision such as this. Make sure that your voice is heard and that you establish a platform to hear the other person's voice as well.

When breaking up, it is equally important to know what not to do. Do not, under any circumstances:

- **Allow yourself to be guilted into holding on to a toxic situation:** Once you have identified a situation as toxic, you can't continue in the situation for fear of hurting your partner. Although it is unfortunate that you may hurt their feelings along the way, remember, pain is temporary. The big picture is your happiness and if someone is getting in the way of that, you must remove them from your life.

- **Stay without having a plan:** Sometimes, honest conversations can lead to renewed feelings of positivity and hope. This is perfectly fine! However, if you're going to stay, you must have a plan. It is careless to proceed without agreeing with your partner on how to improve in certain areas that are lacking.

- **Engage in a battle of accusations:** In romantic relationships, it is easy to remove blame from yourself and place it on your partner. However, it rarely matters who is at fault. What matters instead is the ability of two people to work together, recognize issues, address them, and move forward to the benefit of both. An environment in which this isn't achievable is toxic and should be ended immediately. It does no good for anyone to play the "blame game."

Ultimately, situations that require breakups are never ideal. They tend to involve pain, regret, and hurt feelings. However, it is important to remember someone else's happiness must never come at the expense of your own. The way you treat yourself sets the standard for how everyone else will treat you. If you're not willing to place yourself first, even when things get tough, then no one else will either.

-

CHAPTER 3

THE KEY
TAKEAWAYS

There is no right or a wrong way to motivate yourself. There is no version of yourself that is "bad" to aspire to be. There is no one philosophy or ideology that will necessarily produce results in your life. All these things are entirely dependent on you as a person and the nature of your journey. The principles and practices in this book are not designed to give you one single method of winning your race and becoming your best self. People are not so generic as to be able to apply **one** methodology to achieve their goals. Instead, *Winning Your Race* was designed to present several beneficial practices and ideas you can apply to your current regimen.

Think of the knowledge in this book as you would nutrition supplements. By design, supplements are not intended to replace your normal diet or work-out routine. However, when you take supplements in conjunction with a healthy diet and work-out plan, you will amplify your results to a profound degree. The way you take them is dependent on your work-out routine, your diet, and your body. If you take the knowledge in this book along with the methods that work the best to accomplish your goals, you will maximize your results enormously over time.

You can tackle your mission toward personal progression in just as many ways as you can tackle fitness. However, there are some universal rules that govern any fitness journey. For example, you should always drink plenty of water, get ample sleep, and pursue your fitness goals within the realm of what you are physically capable of achieving. Consider the following key takeaways for your life journey just as you would the universal rules for a fitness journey. If you take heed to *anything* in this book, take heed to the takeaways in this chapter.

THE ENEMY WITHIN

"I stopped fighting my inner demons. We're on the same side now."
–Darynda Jones, *Second Grave on the Left*

Before you get into this chapter, make sure you have spent time with self-reflection and self-acceptance (Chapters 1 and 2). Attempts to address the Enemy Within without an appropriate level of self-understanding will not result in your favor. Consider this scenario:

> There is a version of yourself that you do not like. You sit alone and think of moments in your past that you are not proud of, and they make you cringe, even now. Times when you did not say what you should have, or you acted in a way that you are not proud of–all remind you of the qualities you possess that you cannot stand.

> There exists a side of you that you do not want to share with the world, the side of you that will lie in bed for days at a time watching movies, eating unhealthy food, unsure of what to do next or how to do it.

There is a side of you that you would do any-thing to get rid of. It is the source of your in-securities—that part of yourself that you blame for all your shortcomings, failures, and personal disappointments.

It's the part of yourself that makes you ashamed of yourself sometimes. It's the side of yourself that you are working, sometimes desperately, to improve. This is the Enemy Within.

WHERE DOES THE "ENEMY WITHIN" COME FROM?

The most difficult part of self-acceptance is embracing the characteristics of yourself that you do not like—the character-istics that you do not think *anyone* likes—and moving forward with a sense of wholeness and fulfillment.

The easiest way to identify the Enemy Within is by re-flecting on past embarrassing experiences. Take a moment to recall an embarrassing moment from your past when you did something that made a group of people upset or something they mocked you for. In that moment and every time that you reflect on that moment, you are overcome with distaste at *whatever* quality within you caused it. Consider this example: You were tasked with delivering a speech, and you performed terribly. You wish that you were the type of person who was more capable of handling situations such as that under pressure or thinking quickly on your feet. You can't help but resent that part of yourself that seems to fall short in the public eye, and you regret that you were not the person you needed to be in that moment.

When faced with this type of difficulty, it is easy for people to separate their ideal self from the qualities they feel led to their failure. This leads to the development of the Enemy Within. Within you is your Ideal Self—the self you would like to be or how you see yourself. The Ideal Self consists of your favorite things about yourself. Then you have the Enemy Within, which consists of the undesirable qualities that we tend to feel hold us back from the Ideal Self.

"If you know the enemy and know yourself, you need not fear the result of a hundred battles."
—Sun Tzu, Strategist

HOW DO YOU BEAT THE ENEMY WITHIN?

Think of yourself as a sculpture, placed in the center of a plaza. Depending on where a person is standing, they may have an entirely different view of you. Their view is based on their perspective and is completely out of your control.

In most instances, your Ideal Self and the Enemy Within are separate from one another. You work to make sure people are only exposed to your Ideal Self, since it is your best side. While this sounds reasonable, it is illogical. Think back to the sculpture: It would not make sense to ask that people only stand on one side of the plaza to view the sculpture from the best angle. It would also be nonsensical for a sculptor to design a sculpture that only looked good from a certain viewpoint, knowing it will be placed in a centralized location! In this example, the Enemy Within is represented by the sides of the sculpture that appear to be undeveloped or unfinished depending on where a person stands in the plaza.

1. **Identify the Enemy Within.** Take the time to identify the parts of yourself that you are not fond of or that you know you wish people were not aware of. Become familiar with the side of yourself that you wish to keep hidden and the reasons why you feel this way.

2. **Embrace the Enemy Within.** You must acknowledge your shortcomings as a part of your personality. The best parts of yourself would not exist without the Enemy Within. Once you have acknowledged your flaws, decide which ones you can work to change. As for the ones that you cannot change? Embrace both. *It is as simple as that.* Make no mistake, things that are simple are not necessarily easy, but they are not difficult to comprehend. If you have a problem with your weight, take active steps to change it. If

you have a problem with your height, embrace it because it was never in your control, nor will it be. Choose instead to love that part of yourself more than anyone has before.

"The supreme art of war is to subdue the enemy without fighting."
– Sun Tzu, *The Art of War*

3. **The Final Step: End the Conflict Within Yourself.** Until you realize your full potential, you are a work-in-progress. You are allowed to be unfinished. In your journey to self-fulfillment and the fulfillment of your purpose, you are allowed to be flawed. You are allowed to fall short of certain goals. You are allowed to fail. Accept that these "shortcomings" are a natural and necessary part of your path, and the negative feelings you have toward certain aspects of yourself will fade away.

Turn once again to the analogy of the sculpture in the plaza. It is impossible to peel beautiful portions of the sculpture away from portions that may be considered unflattering. An artist does not seek to do this. It is the combination of every part of the sculpture–its cohesiveness as well its contrasting nature–that makes it a beautiful piece of art, which can be appreciated and celebrated from all angles. You are no different. Author Julia Hill shares these insights on the transformation process:

True transformation occurs only when we can look at ourselves squarely and face our attachments and inner demons, free from the buzz of commercial distraction and false social realities. We have to retreat into our own cocoons and come face-to-face with who we are. We have to turn toward our own inner darkness. For only by abandoning its attachments and facing the darkness does the caterpillar's body begin to spread out, and its light, beautiful wings begin to form.

LOVING YOURSELF

"Peace is our original state . . . new Beginnings are often disguised as painful endings."
–Lao Tzu, Philosopher

Regardless of how much success you encounter, it can be difficult to fight off feelings of inadequacy. Even in your moments of blissful celebration, you have a constant fear of giving yourself too much credit. People around you are incredibly impressed with the things you do, and although you accept their praise, you don't mirror their sentiments.

Your constant desire to improve yourself and achieve "more" has you feeling as if right now, you aren't good enough. You criticize yourself with incredible harshness and often don't feel as if you're doing as well as people think you are.

To make matters worse, the people around you are doing amazing things all the time! At times, it feels like you are never quite where you want

to be, no matter how great others think of you;
even though you wouldn't describe yourself as
having low self-esteem, you wouldn't say it was
high either. Something is missing, and you can-
not quite place your finger on what it is.

Your self-love is incredibly lacking.

HOW DO YOU FIX IT?

We are constantly assaulted with influences that teach us to love certain things in people. Whether the focus is on a physical appearance, natural talent, class, status, it often falls on things that are out of your control. For example, an artist like Alicia Keys is applauded for her talent but never for her humanitarian efforts that she leads in Africa. Or an athlete like LeBron James is celebrated for his superhuman athleticism but never for his business smarts. People are often celebrated for things that they *cannot* control. If you allow these things to influence your perception of yourself, or even other people, then you can often draw conclusions about things that are misleading. When we think of ourselves, it is not with the same admiration that is given to the widely popular people who we have grown to adore. That's because we are only told to admire external factors, factors that are often out of people's control. It is much more uncommon that people celebrate things like kindness, character, a giving spirit, work ethic, study habits, or any other factors that fall under a person's control. It is easy to forget about these characteristics, the ones that really matter.

Consider for a moment the reason that your mother loves you. It is not because you are tall or short, it is not because of your weight, it is not because of your money. It has never been about things like that, and it never will be. It is because your mother, just like everyone close to you, has had the opportunity to see you as who you really are. Through your highest and lowest moments, the people close to you have been witnesses to your true character, and that has led them to love you. The people in your life, who've given you undying loyalty, endless sacrifice, and limitless sacrifice, love you because they've seen you at your most powerful as well as your most vulnerable. Through accurate self-reflection, you can achieve the same view of yourself. The author JoyBell C. describes some of the benefits of self-reflection this way:

> The person in life that you will always be with the most, is yourself. Because even when you are with others, you are still with yourself, too! When you wake up in the morning, you are with yourself, lying in bed at night you are with yourself, walking down the street in the sunlight you are with yourself. What kind of person do you want to walk down the street with? What kind of person do you want to wake up in the morning with? What kind of person do you

want to see at the end of the day before you fall asleep? Because that person is yourself, and it's your responsibility to be that person you want to be with. I know I want to spend my life with a person who knows how to let things go, who's not full of hate, who's able to smile and be carefree. So that's who I have to be.

Take the time to spend time with yourself. Meditate, be a little lazy, do ONLY the things that you like, shop, listen to music. Discover yourself, fully, better than anyone ever has before. As you start to become more in tune with the person that you are, you will begin to love yourself boundlessly. And if you don't like the person that you are, you can ALWAYS work to grow into a better version of yourself.

After you have accepted yourself, there is no end to what you can accomplish. By removing barriers between you and your truest self, you eliminate the inhibitions that stop you from achieving all your wildest goals.

A WORD ON FRIENDSHIP

There is nothing more sacred in the world than the relationship you share with a true friend. Family is important, but you are never afforded the opportunity to choose your family, only your friends. I belong to an international fraternity (Omega Psi Phi Fraternity, Incorporated) whose motto is "Friendship is Essential to the Soul." The nature, costs, value, and qualities of a friend are thoroughly examined, disputed, and discussed by the members of my organization on a constant basis.

We tend to fall under the impression that friendships should only be the result of organic, coincidental interaction. Subsequently, we maintain the idea that friendships should require minimal effort, compromise, or sacrifice on our part. As commonplace as these expectations are, they are baseless and inaccurate. Friendships, successfully cultivated, require a healthy amount of attention to detail to maintain. No garden will bear fruit without proper care and attention. The same can be said for a friendship.

"Friendship is always a sweet responsibility, never an opportunity."
−Khalil Gibran, Lebanese Writer

The members of my fraternity have taught me several lessons about friendship, some easier to learn than others. I've learned that everyone isn't always deserving of your friendship, even if they want it. Accountability is an important part of friendship, although it can be painful at times. Friends don't always provide you with the things you want, but they'll sacrifice to get you the things you need. A friend will require that you remain at your best. Although you choose your friends, you don't choose *when* to be a friend; friendship will call on you at inconvenient times. Friends never count favors. You never have to plead for authenticity from a friend. Most importantly, friendships are filled with reciprocity. Although the things friends do for one another may differ in value, the mutual feeling of fulfillment is unquestionable.

Take care when choosing your friends; they will be there for you through the most trying of circumstances. The worst act one can commit is to take a friend for granted. Remain wary so that you are never on the wrong side of friendship.

LEADERSHIP AND WHAT IT MEANS

Leadership is a necessary component for most successes. It is the spark to an otherwise useless tinder that we call "potential." It is ambition's most reactive catalyst. When the right person exercises leadership, they can accomplish things previously considered to be impossible. However, because of the overwhelming amount of acknowledgement and accolades that leaders receive as well as the misconception that a leader is the best person in each group, there is overwhelming pressure on people to step into leadership. Usually, this push to become a leader (whether from within or from a high-pressure environment) comes before a person has had adequate timing to develop into a leader on their own.

Leadership, by definition, requires a following. The single most effective way to learn to lead is to follow a great leader. There is nothing wrong with being a follower; it is a necessary step along the journey toward developing an effective understanding of leadership. Consider a leader who has a superb follower, a shining example of things the leader strives to achieve. The follower, in their own way, is just as much of a leader as the actual leader. The leader's other followers will base their behavior on that of the superb follower, mimicking the qualities that have been identified as beneficial for bringing the leader's vision into fruition. Though the position of a superb follower denotes leadership, it is seldom celebrated or acknowledged.

I am a member of the United States Armed Forces, currently serving on active duty. There is no organization that boasts a more effective understanding of leadership than the American military. Every member of the Armed Forces falls into one of three categories: one who creates policy, one who enforces policy, or one who abides by the policies. Those who create policy are tasked with creating policies that bring success to the organization on a holistic level. They must create a vision that, if adhered to, will ensure the organization's well-being. They require the aid of those who enforce policy; without enforcers, policymakers would not have the appropriate amount of time to dedicate to constructing their vision. Enforcers ensure that the policy is abided by, and those who abide by the policy carry out the tasks necessary to keep the organization afloat and thriving. Each of these roles is tasked to the individuals who are most suited to carry them out. There are leaders and subordinates within each category of military personnel, and each category has specific rewards for commendable behavior.

This system, which the United States has meticulously cultivated, not only encourages leadership, but it also cultivates it. It does so by illuminating the single most important component selfto lead by: self-determination. Self-determination can be boiled down to deciding things for yourself, by yourself (essentially, a person with self-determination is their **own** leader).

Leadership does not always come with a slew of accolades and acknowledgements. Leading does not always consist of standing at the forefront and issuing commands. However, indubitably, leadership consists of self-determination. The self-motivated, self-driven, and self-led individual is invaluable, no matter what circumstances they are placed in. In any situation, they will blaze their own trail toward the achievement of their goals.

AN OPEN LETTER TO THE "OVERLY" AMBITIOUS

There is no such thing as overly ambitious . . .

> You probably push yourself harder than anyone you know. You probably get over your accomplishments as soon as you are rewarded for them.

> You probably compare yourself to highly successful people and feel inadequate. You are probably hardly satisfied with yourself, if ever.

> This quality that you have about yourself comes with an incredible duality. There is the obvious: you're rarely happy with your completed work or projects. You probably feel isolated from your friends and family at times. Others often say you "do too much" when it comes to your dedication to your goals. You have been called "obsessed."

All of this is perfectly acceptable. Understand this: No one can want things for you as bad as you want them for yourself. People who do not pursue their goals as aggressively as you will not relate to the pressure that you apply to yourself. They have a hard time understanding that you are unhappy with anything except the best and are incredibly dissatisfied with ever coming in second place at anything.

The duality of your incredible ambition is clear: On one hand, you will have to walk your path alone at times because most people simply cannot understand you. On the other hand, you possess the capability to push yourself to heights that others can only imagine.

Your journey will be adverse, but remember: *Every adverse situation that you encounter is an opportunity for you to become better.*

REWARD YOURSELF

Remember that your high levels of ambition will not always be understood by your peers; only you will truly comprehend the various components of your journey. It is important that *you* make the effort to reward yourself for hitting important milestones along your path lest they go unnoticed.

You've heard about the importance of self-reward countless times, but you tend to stay away from it. We all know an abundance of people who seem to *always* celebrate and spend money on things in the name of "rewarding themselves," but never seem to do anything productive. *You are not like them.*

When you reward yourself, you don't need acknowledgement or approval from others to keep you going. All you need is your own focus and drive to achieve all the things you want.

EMBRACE THE PROCESS

Your journey is a beautiful one. It will be incredibly challenging, but even more rewarding. Throughout its best and worst moments, you must embrace it fully. Your attitude shapes your perspective, and your perspective ultimately determines your reality. The pain of running a race is only surpassed by the thrill of emerging as the victor. Understand that these two elements—the pain and the thrill—cannot exist separately from one another. Master this balance and you will find that you tackle even the most difficult tasks with a victorious spirit.

"If there is no struggle, there is no progress."
—Frederick Douglass, Orator

You're going after everything you deserve. Your journey will be filled with challenges, and in those most trying moments, remember that *wanting it is never enough.* Now that you've made a decision to have something most people won't have, you have to do things most people won't do.

Most importantly, keep going. Every single day provides you with endless opportunities to improve yourself, advance your grind, and develop your hustle. Every–Single–Day. Don't ever pass up a chance to step closer to your goals.

Truly Yours

-

100 THINGS TO

KNOW

1. There is nothing wrong with putting yourself first.
2. The weeds take the garden. Stay productive.
3. Promises are like babies—easy to make, hard to deliver.
4. The game is meant to be sold, not told.
5. Fortune favors the bold.
6. Loyalty is hard to come by. Once you find it, don't let it go.
7. Whenever looking to solve a problem, always look within yourself first.
8. Take responsibility for your outcomes; circumstances are out of your hands.
9. No struggle? No progress.
10. The best medicine is usually bitter.
11. Only take advice from people who have the things that you want.
12. Take the time to appreciate your circumstances. Most situations are temporary.
13. The place where you fit may not exist until you create it.
14. The most rewarding things are on the other side of fear.
15. You will only go so far as you believe that you can.
16. Behavior is the only proof of motivation.
17. Read every day.
18. Challenge yourself in all the things that you do.
19. Take pride in small works.
20. Remind people close to you that you care for them.
21. Convictions, firmly held, will always cost you.
22. Learn to do that which stops most people.
23. It's not what you make; it's what you keep.

24. The best way to ensure success is to deserve it.
25. Know when to quit and when to keep going it.
26. A bad hand doesn't mean the game is lost.
27. Perspective is everything, and you can never have too much of it.
28. Sometimes, what it *is* matters just as much as how it *looks*.
29. Tell yourself what you want to be, and then do what it takes to get there.
30. You cannot be *everything* to *everyone*.
31. Cleanliness is next to godliness.
32. Patience is the seed that always bears fruit.
33. There is nothing so fulfilling as dedicating your efforts to something larger than yourself.
34. You are the sum of your thoughts and actions.
35. Lift as you climb.
36. The fruit will fall when it is ripe, do not disturb it.
37. Too much of any good thing is soon a bad thing.
38. A mind unchallenged is a mind wasted.
39. Find your lane and stay in it. If there is not one? Make one.
40. Comparison will steal your joy.
41. Tomorrow is a land of unfulfilled promises and unfinished work. Do it now.
42. There is good in anything if you look for it.
43. Be polite to all, casual to many, familiar with a few, and friendly to a handful.
44. You can't argue ignorance away; only knowledge can cure ignorance.

45. Preparation is the mother of good fortune.
46. No one wants you to succeed as bad as you do.
47. When things seem hopeless, your situation can only improve.
48. If you look forward, you will head forward. Let the past go.
49. You cannot build a skyscraper on a foundation meant for a house.
50. In order to have more, you have to do more.
51. Luck favors the well-prepared and the hard working.
52. Money saved is money earned.
53. You can never put a price on time. Use it wisely.
54. Don't lose sight of the forest for the trees.
55. Don't lose sight of the trees for the forest.
56. Focus on yourself first; everything else will work itself out.
57. Be not afraid of going slowly, only of standing still.
58. Take heed to the way you feel; your emotions tell truths that reason cannot.
59. Take yourself seriously, but not too seriously.
60. There are always ways to improve yourself; never settle for good enough.
61. You will be amazed at how fast you travel when you are in your own lane.
62. Do not allow anyone to tell you how something should make you feel.
63. There has never been a passionate person who hasn't thought about giving up.
64. The day that you cease to amaze yourself is the day that

you're done.

65. Good things come to those who wait, not to those who are lazy.

66. You can do anything that you decide you are going to do.

67. No one cares about your problems more than you do; don't be fooled and think that people care about why you're complaining.

68. There is such a thing as fake love.

69. Be wary of those who only associate once the work is done.

70. The journey is just as important as the destination.

71. If you don't, then who will?

72. You are the only thing that you're afraid of.

73. Do not feel bad for people who are uncomfortable when you shine your own light.

74. Respect is earned not given.

75. You won't get acknowledgment for just being present; add to the space.

76. Leave every space you enter better than how you found it.

77. Rashness breeds misfortune.

78. Never love something so much that you are unwilling to walk away from it.

79. People will tell you everything you need to know about them if you let them.

80. Where you focus your energy is where you will see results.

81. Greatness is not what you do occasionally, but what you do consistently.

82. Accept inspiration from all sources in life.

83. You don't have to show it to the world for it to be true.

84. Imitation is the highest form of humility.

85. You are not obligated to explain yourself to anyone.

86. There is only one truth, but there are several sides to it.

87. It is easier to keep up than catch up.

88. Some tigers are better left wild.

89. Always do more than what is expected of you.

90. Healthy competition is incredibly productive.

91. Never blame someone for being the way that they are.

92. Follow your bliss.

93. Trust yourself above all else.

94. Nothing in life is free.

95. Your perspective belongs to you and only you.

96. Never rush people to understand you.

97. Every well runs dry.

98. Empty yourself of negative thoughts on a regular basis.

99. Positivity is a process not just a perspective.

100. You are the most important person who has ever lived. Your existence is a miracle. Put it to use.

-

QUOTE
COLLECTION

"Examination of our past is never time-wasting. Reverberations from the past provide learning rubrics for living today."
−Kilroy J. Oldster, Author

"Even if you think you're doing well and have it all figured out, there is a voice you will always inevitably hear at some point which nags at you and says, "but wait..." Don't ever dismiss it, listen to what it has to say. Life will never be close enough to perfect, and listening to that voice means stepping outside of yourself and considering your own wrongdoings and flaws."
−Ashly Lorenzana, Digital Content Creator

"Everything in your life, from your diet to your career, must be aligned with your purpose. If you know your purpose, your deepest desire, then the secret of success is to discipline your life so that you support your deepest purpose."
−David Deida, Author

"Failure should be our teacher, not our undertaker. Failure is delay, not defeat. It is a temporary detour, not a dead end. Failure is something we can avoid only by saying nothing, doing nothing, and being nothing."
−Denis Waitley, Author; Motivational Speaker

"Success is stumbling from failure to failure with no loss of enthusiasm."
−Winston Churchill

"Never had to ask a lot 'cause I went and did it; If you lazy then I doubt that you would get it."
−LE$, Hip-Hop Artist

"Of course, motivation is not permanent. But then, neither is bathing; but it is something you should do on a regular basis."
−Zig Ziglar, Author

"Friendship is always a sweet responsibility, never an opportunity."

—Khalil Gibran, Lebanese Writer

"*Believe in yourself, your abilities and your own potential. Never let self-doubt hold you captive. You are worthy of all that you dream of and hope for.*"
—Roy Bennett

"*Once we accept our limits, we go beyond them.*"
—Albert Einstein

"*Grow in happiness . . . and you'll glow in this peaceful way. Your friends will be very, very happy with you. Everyone will want to sit next to you. And people will give you money!*"
—David Lynch, Filmmaker

"*Giving thanks, recognizing all the good in your life, is the gateway drug to a life most extraordinary. It's the superpower that moves you onto the frequency where beauty and joy and creativity happen.*"

—Pam Grout, author of *Thank and Grow Rich*

"As I began to love myself I freed myself of anything that is no good for my health–food, people, things, situations, and everything that drew me down and away from myself. At first, I called this attitude a healthy egoism. Today I know it is 'LOVE OF ONESELF.'"
—Charlie Chaplin

"how you love yourself is how you teach others to love you"
—Rupi Kaur, Poet

"Expectations are dangerous when they are both too high and uninformed."
—Lionel Shriver, Author

"Expectations are like fine pottery. The harder you hold them, the more likely they are to crack."
—Brandon Sanderson, Author

"To share your weakness is to make yourself vulnerable; to make yourself vulnerable is to show your strength."
—Criss Jami, Poet

"Vulnerability is the birthplace of love, belonging, joy, courage, empathy, and creativity. It is the source of hope, empathy, accountability, and authenticity. If we want greater clarity in our purpose and more meaningful, spiritual lives, vulnerability is the path."
—Brene Brown, Author

"There is no more miserable human being than one in whom nothing is habitual but indecision."
—William James, Philosopher

"Allow people to know your wants, needs and desires in their most natural form."
—Diamond Dorris, Digital Content Producer

"Your task is not to seek for love, but merely to seek and find all the barriers within yourself that you have built against it."
–Jalaluddin Rumi, 13th Century Persian Poet & Philosopher

"If you are waiting for anything in order to live and love without holding back, then you suffer. Every moment is the most important moment of your life."
–David Deida, Author

"I stopped fighting my inner demons. We're on the same side now."
–Darynda Jones, *Second Grave on the Left*

"If you know the enemy and know yourself, you need not fear the result of a hundred battles."
–Sun Tzu, Strategist

"True transformation occurs only when we can look at ourselves squarely and face our attachments and inner demons, free from the buzz of commercial distraction and false social realities. We have to retreat into our own cocoons and come face-to-face with who we are. We have to turn toward our own inner darkness. For only by abandoning its attachments and facing the darkness does the caterpillar's body begin to spread out, and its light, beautiful wings begin to form."

—Julia Hill, Author

"Authenticity is a collection of choices that we have to make every day. The choice to let our true selves be seen."

—Brene Brown, Author

"Build a bond first, don't force anything. A person's actions will tell you everything you need to know."

—40oz Van, Digital Content Creator, Social Influencer

"Care about what other people think and you will always be their prisoner."
−Lao Tzu, Philosopher

"Peace is our original state . . . new Beginnings are often disguised as painful endings."
−Lao Tzu, Philosopher

"It's a marathon, not a sprint. Constant repetition is the path to progression."
−Nipsey Hussle, Hip-Hop Artist, Entrepreneur

"It's not what we do once in a while that shapes our lives. It's what we do consistently."
−Tony Robbins

"People who are unable to motivate themselves must be content with mediocrity, no matter how impressive their other talents."
−Andrew Carnegie, Philanthropist

THE BOTTOM LINES

CHAPTER 1: DO IT FOR YOU

- Successful relationships, successful careers, successful family lives, and success in general all share an underlying trait: they do not occur by accident. Only once you have an accurate self-image can you begin to understand what things work for you in life and what things do not. This practice will align you with your life's purpose and place you on your most important journey: the journey from the person you ARE to the person you would LIKE to become.

- Whether you call it your grind, your hustle, or your daily routine, it does not matter. What does matter is that you are relentless in accomplishing the things that you resolve to do. Outwork yourself every day. Start small, and eventually you will see that even gargantuan tasks crumble beneath your unwavering discipline.

- Remember, it may not be easy to define what your life's purpose is. For some people, it is not as simple as playing basketball or writing songs. However, regardless of your passions, being the best version of yourself is ALWAYS a part of your purpose. Don't lose sight of being your best self, and never allow your circumstances to define who you are!

- Failure is a natural and necessary part of success. Success without failure isn't commendable; it is luck. Embrace the hard times and adverse situations that your journey will bring you to; they only result in your improvement and a deepened appreciation of your eventual successes.

- Maintaining your motivation is a simple, easily forgotten task that will separate you from the masses. This practice will take your work ethic from "good" to "unbelievable" with the simple application of a few techniques. Imagine a vehicle that could fuel itself based on pure willpower. There are no boundaries to where it could travel. You are no different; be your own fuel.

- Your journey is too important to allow roadblocks that you created to slow down your progress. Keep in mind that you will always be your first critic, and your most harsh. Remember, you are the only critic that you must prove wrong. Your self-doubts will always fall short of your consistent progression.

- It is a hard truth to face for some—the truth that "all that positivity nonsense" isn't quite nonsense. It is also daunting to consider that you are solely responsible for your own happiness. Consider yourself during a time when you were happy and working; you were most likely alive with productive energy and fruitful passion. If you could have this level of enthusiasm all the time, your limits would fall away. The world belongs to those who love living in it.

CHAPTER 2: DO IT FOR THE LOVE

- After you have accepted yourself, there is no end to what you can accomplish. By removing barriers between you and your truest self, you eliminate the inhibitions that stop you from receiving the love from others that you deserve.

- The time you take to manage your expectations will only create more time for you to work towards more desirable outcomes. There are two generally accepted solutions to creating more happiness: lowering your expectations or improving your reality. Expectation management will help you achieve the latter.

- Vulnerability is no simple thing to demand of yourself. It takes an incredible amount of self-trust and self-acceptance to be comfortable revealing things others would consider shortcomings. However, once you make a habit of doing so, you will find yourself with a level of empowerment unmatched by anything you have felt before. Once you have chosen to share your true self with the world, nothing is off limits to you.

- When your lifestyle is focused on your personal development and betterment, it does not make sense to interrupt that for a person who shows strong potential. Anyone or anything can show strong potential if your imagination is active enough. I encourage you to take a more realistic, casual approach to getting to know your potential partners so that you can reap the benefits of authentic romantic bonds.

- Unfortunately, when it comes to unique feelings such as the Settling Anxiety, there is no one size fits all solution. At times, many things won't seem to work. However, once you are fully in tune with yourself, you will always be able to identify why you feel certain things. Self-reflection is always a great first step. The distress that you and your partner face and conquer will always strengthen your bond.

- Ultimately, situations that require breakups are never ideal. They tend to involve pain, regret, and hurt feelings. However, it is important to remember someone else's happiness can never come at the expense of your own. The way you treat yourself sets the standard for how everyone else will treat you. If you're not willing to place yourself first, even when things get tough, then no one else will either.

CHAPTER 3: THE KEY TAKEAWAYS

- "True transformation occurs only when we can look at ourselves squarely and face our attachments and inner demons, free from the buzz of commercial distraction and false social realities. We have to retreat into our own cocoons and come face-to-face with who we are. We have to turn toward our own inner darkness. For only by abandoning its attachments and facing the darkness does the caterpillar's body begin to spread out, and its light, beautiful wings begin to form." –Julia Hill

- After you have accepted yourself, there is no end to what you can accomplish. By removing barriers between you and your truest self, you eliminate the inhibitions that stop you from achieving all of your wildest goals.

-

QUESTIONS FOR SELF-REFLECTION

This list is here purely to aid in some of your journaling and self-reflection. Ask yourself the tough questions so that your self-image is as accurate as possible. Progress begins within.

- How do I feel about myself?

- What are my best/worst qualities?

- When is the last time I made myself proud?

- How do other people view my behavior?

- Why did I choose my friends?

- What am I doing to work toward my goals?

- Am I satisfied with myself?

- Are there things about myself I wish I could change?

- What is my biggest regret? Was it my fault?

- Do I accept full responsibility for my current situation

- Is my view of myself consistent with how others view me?

- When do I feel the most/least comfortable?

- How much do I care about the opinions of others?

- Am I an effective communicator?

- What truly motivates me?

- Am I satisfied by my personal relationships (i.e., friend-ships/romantic relationships)?

- What do I do to cope with my problems?

- Do I handle conflict effectively?

- Am I in control of my circumstances?

- When do I feel the most joy?

- What are my biggest mistakes?

- What inspires me the most?

- Where do I find comfort in hard times?

- Do people value my time?

- What is my biggest shortcoming?

- What is my greatest asset?

- Why do people like me?

- Do I deserve my current situation?

- If I weren't myself, would I like me?

-

SUGGESTED
READINGS AND
SOURCES OF
INFLUENCE

- ## DAVID DEIDA, AUTHOR
  Official Website: https://deida.info
  Suggested Reading: The Way of the Superior Man, Blue Truth

- ## LE$, HIP-HOP ARTIST
  Official Website: http://www.steakxshrimp.com
  Suggested Listening: E36, Expansion Pack, (all his projects, really).
  Social Media Handles: Twitter/Instagram - @steakxshrimp

- ## PAM GROUT, AUTHOR
  Official Website: https://pamgrout.com/bio/
  Suggested Reading: Thank & Grow Rich
  Social Media Handles: Twitter - @PamGrout

- ## DIAMOND DORRIS, DIGITAL CONTENT PRODUCER
  Official Website: http://lovethediosa.com
  Social Media Handles: Twitter/Instagram - @lovethediosa

- ## SUN TZU, STRATEGIST
  Suggested Reading: The Art of War

- ## 40OZ VAN, DIGITAL CONTENT CREATOR, SOCIAL INFLUENCER
  Social Media Handles: Twitter/Instagram: @40oz_VAN

- ## NIPSEY HUSSLE, HIP-HOP ARTIST, ENTREPRENEUR
  Official Website: https://www.themarathonclothing.com
  Suggested Listening: The Marathon, Mailbox Money (all his
  music is worth giving a listen).
  Social Media Handles: Twitter/Instagram - @NipseyHussle

- ## LAO TZU, PHILOSOPHER
  Suggested Reading: Tao Te Ching (The Way and its Power)

CPSIA information can be obtained
at www.ICGtesting.com
Printed in the USA
BVHW03s1912200418
514004BV00003B/11/P

9 780692 077283